- THE -
ULTIMATE
- DIVE -

Log Book

Name

DIVE NO

DATE

DIVE GROUP

WEATHER CONDITIONS

START
bar / psi

END
bar / psi

LOCATION

TIME IN

TIME OUT

:

:

DIVE TIME

:

AVERAGE DEPTH

MAX DEPTH

ADDITIONAL NOTES

WEATHER CONDITIONS

LOCATION

LOCATION NAME

COUNTRY

EQUIPMENT

DIVE CENTER / RESORT STAMP

INSTRUCTOR

AI / DM

BUDDY

DIVE NO

DATE

DIVE GROUP

WEATHER CONDITIONS

START
bar / psi

END
bar / psi

LOCATION

TIME IN

TIME OUT

:

:

DIVE TIME

:

AVERAGE DEPTH

MAX DEPTH

ADDITIONAL NOTES

WEATHER CONDITIONS

LOCATION

LOCATION NAME

COUNTRY

EQUIPMENT

DIVE CENTER / RESORT STAMP

INSTRUCTOR

AI / DM

BUDDY

DIVE NO

DATE

DIVE GROUP

WEATHER CONDITIONS

START
bar / psi

END
bar / psi

LOCATION

TIME IN

TIME OUT

:

:

DIVE TIME

:

AVERAGE DEPTH

MAX DEPTH

ADDITIONAL NOTES

WEATHER CONDITIONS

LOCATION

LOCATION NAME

COUNTRY

EQUIPMENT

DIVE CENTER / RESORT STAMP

INSTRUCTOR

AI / DM

BUDDY

DIVE NO

DATE

DIVE GROUP

WEATHER CONDITIONS

WEATHER CONDITIONS

START bar / psi	END bar / psi

LOCATION

LOCATION NAME

COUNTRY

LOCATION

TIME IN

:

TIME OUT

:

DIVE TIME

:

AVERAGE DEPTH

MAX DEPTH

EQUIPMENT

ADDITIONAL NOTES

DIVE CENTER / RESORT STAMP

INSTRUCTOR

AI / DM

BUDDY

DIVE NO

DATE

DIVE GROUP

WEATHER CONDITIONS

START bar / psi	END bar / psi

LOCATION

TIME IN

:

TIME OUT

:

DIVE TIME

:

AVERAGE DEPTH

MAX DEPTH

ADDITIONAL NOTES

WEATHER CONDITIONS

☐ ☐ ☐ ☐ ☐

LOCATION

LOCATION NAME

COUNTRY

EQUIPMENT

DIVE CENTER / RESORT STAMP

INSTRUCTOR   AI / DM   BUDDY

☐   ☐   ☐

DIVE NO

DATE

DIVE GROUP

WEATHER CONDITIONS

WEATHER CONDITIONS

START
bar / psi

END
bar / psi

LOCATION

TIME IN

TIME OUT

:

:

DIVE TIME

:

AVERAGE DEPTH

MAX DEPTH

LOCATION

LOCATION NAME

COUNTRY

EQUIPMENT

ADDITIONAL NOTES

DIVE CENTER / RESORT STAMP

INSTRUCTOR

AI / DM

BUDDY

DIVE NO

DATE

DIVE GROUP

WEATHER CONDITIONS

WEATHER CONDITIONS

START
bar / psi

END
bar / psi

LOCATION

TIME IN

TIME OUT

:

:

DIVE TIME

:

AVERAGE DEPTH

MAX DEPTH

LOCATION

LOCATION NAME

COUNTRY

EQUIPMENT

ADDITIONAL NOTES

DIVE CENTER / RESORT STAMP

INSTRUCTOR

AI / DM

BUDDY

DIVE NO

DATE

DIVE GROUP

WEATHER CONDITIONS

START
bar / psi
_____

END
bar / psi
_____

LOCATION

TIME IN

TIME OUT

:

:

DIVE TIME

:

AVERAGE DEPTH

MAX DEPTH

ADDITIONAL NOTES

WEATHER CONDITIONS

_____

_____

LOCATION

LOCATION NAME

COUNTRY

EQUIPMENT

DIVE CENTER / RESORT STAMP

INSTRUCTOR

AI / DM

BUDDY

DIVE NO

DATE

DIVE GROUP

WEATHER CONDITIONS

START
bar / psi

END
bar / psi

LOCATION

TIME IN

TIME OUT

:

:

DIVE TIME

:

AVERAGE DEPTH

MAX DEPTH

ADDITIONAL NOTES

WEATHER CONDITIONS

—

—

LOCATION

LOCATION NAME

COUNTRY

EQUIPMENT

DIVE CENTER / RESORT STAMP

INSTRUCTOR   AI / DM   BUDDY

DIVE NO

DATE

DIVE GROUP

WEATHER CONDITIONS

WEATHER CONDITIONS

START
bar / psi

END
bar / psi

LOCATION

TIME IN

TIME OUT

:

:

DIVE TIME

:

AVERAGE DEPTH

MAX DEPTH

LOCATION

LOCATION NAME

COUNTRY

EQUIPMENT

ADDITIONAL NOTES

DIVE CENTER / RESORT STAMP

INSTRUCTOR

AI / DM

BUDDY

DIVE NO

DATE

DIVE GROUP

WEATHER CONDITIONS

START
bar / psi

END
bar / psi

LOCATION

TIME IN

TIME OUT

:

:

DIVE TIME

:

AVERAGE DEPTH

MAX DEPTH

ADDITIONAL NOTES

WEATHER CONDITIONS

—

—

LOCATION

LOCATION NAME

COUNTRY

EQUIPMENT

DIVE CENTER / RESORT STAMP

INSTRUCTOR　　　AI / DM　　　BUDDY

DIVE NO

DATE

DIVE GROUP

WEATHER CONDITIONS

START
bar / psi

_____

END
bar / psi

_____

LOCATION

TIME IN

:

TIME OUT

:

DIVE TIME

:

AVERAGE DEPTH

MAX DEPTH

WEATHER CONDITIONS

_____

_____

LOCATION

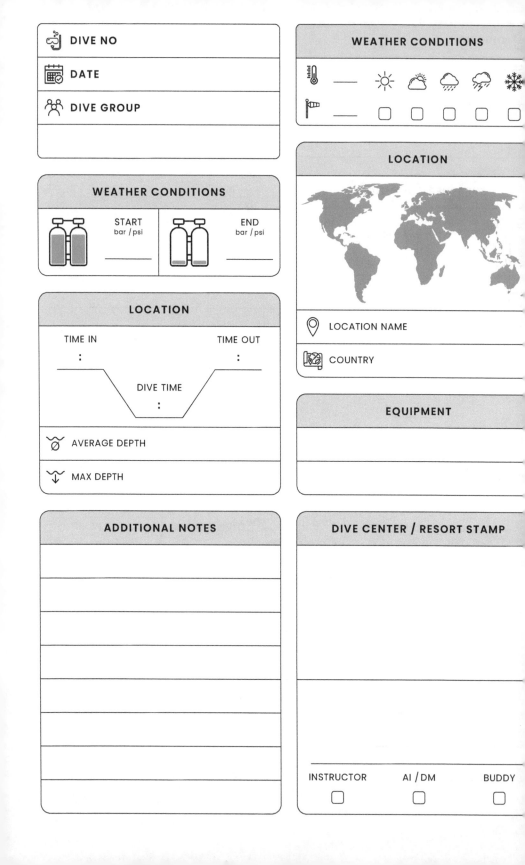

LOCATION NAME

COUNTRY

EQUIPMENT

ADDITIONAL NOTES

DIVE CENTER / RESORT STAMP

INSTRUCTOR

AI / DM

BUDDY

DIVE NO

DATE

DIVE GROUP

WEATHER CONDITIONS

WEATHER CONDITIONS

START
bar / psi

END
bar / psi

_____

_____

LOCATION

TIME IN

TIME OUT

:

:

DIVE TIME

:

AVERAGE DEPTH

MAX DEPTH

LOCATION

LOCATION NAME

COUNTRY

EQUIPMENT

ADDITIONAL NOTES

DIVE CENTER / RESORT STAMP

_____

INSTRUCTOR

AI / DM

BUDDY

DIVE NO

DATE

DIVE GROUP

WEATHER CONDITIONS

WEATHER CONDITIONS

START
bar / psi

END
bar / psi

LOCATION

TIME IN

TIME OUT

:

:

DIVE TIME

:

AVERAGE DEPTH

MAX DEPTH

LOCATION

LOCATION NAME

COUNTRY

EQUIPMENT

ADDITIONAL NOTES

DIVE CENTER / RESORT STAMP

INSTRUCTOR

AI / DM

BUDDY

DIVE NO

DATE

DIVE GROUP

WEATHER CONDITIONS

START
bar / psi

END
bar / psi

WEATHER CONDITIONS

☀ ⛅ ☁ ⛈ ❄

LOCATION

TIME IN   TIME OUT
:   :

DIVE TIME
:

AVERAGE DEPTH

MAX DEPTH

LOCATION

LOCATION NAME

COUNTRY

EQUIPMENT

ADDITIONAL NOTES

DIVE CENTER / RESORT STAMP

INSTRUCTOR   AI / DM   BUDDY

DIVE NO

DATE

DIVE GROUP

WEATHER CONDITIONS

Temperature —

Wind —

WEATHER CONDITIONS

START bar / psi	END bar / psi
_____	_____

LOCATION

LOCATION NAME

COUNTRY

LOCATION

TIME IN :   TIME OUT :

DIVE TIME :

AVERAGE DEPTH

MAX DEPTH

EQUIPMENT

ADDITIONAL NOTES

DIVE CENTER / RESORT STAMP

INSTRUCTOR	AI / DM	BUDDY
☐	☐	☐

DIVE NO

DATE

DIVE GROUP

WEATHER CONDITIONS

———					
———	☐	☐	☐	☐	☐

WEATHER CONDITIONS

START bar / psi	END bar / psi
———	———

LOCATION

⊙ LOCATION NAME

COUNTRY

LOCATION

TIME IN   TIME OUT

:   :

DIVE TIME

:

AVERAGE DEPTH

MAX DEPTH

EQUIPMENT

ADDITIONAL NOTES

DIVE CENTER / RESORT STAMP

INSTRUCTOR	AI / DM	BUDDY
☐	☐	☐

DIVE NO

DATE

DIVE GROUP

WEATHER CONDITIONS

WEATHER CONDITIONS

START
bar / psi
_____

END
bar / psi
_____

LOCATION

TIME IN

:

TIME OUT

:

DIVE TIME

:

AVERAGE DEPTH

MAX DEPTH

LOCATION

LOCATION NAME

COUNTRY

EQUIPMENT

ADDITIONAL NOTES

DIVE CENTER / RESORT STAMP

INSTRUCTOR

AI / DM

BUDDY

DIVE NO

DATE

DIVE GROUP

WEATHER CONDITIONS

☀ ⛅ 🌧 ⛈ ❄
☐ ☐ ☐ ☐ ☐

LOCATION

LOCATION NAME

COUNTRY

WEATHER CONDITIONS

START
bar / psi

END
bar / psi

_____   _____

LOCATION

TIME IN   TIME OUT
    :   :

DIVE TIME
    :

AVERAGE DEPTH

MAX DEPTH

EQUIPMENT

ADDITIONAL NOTES

DIVE CENTER / RESORT STAMP

_____

INSTRUCTOR   AI / DM   BUDDY
    ☐   ☐   ☐

DIVE NO

DATE

DIVE GROUP

WEATHER CONDITIONS

START
bar / psi

END
bar / psi

LOCATION

TIME IN

TIME OUT

:

:

DIVE TIME

:

AVERAGE DEPTH

MAX DEPTH

ADDITIONAL NOTES

WEATHER CONDITIONS

LOCATION

LOCATION NAME

COUNTRY

EQUIPMENT

DIVE CENTER / RESORT STAMP

INSTRUCTOR

AI / DM

BUDDY

DIVE NO

DATE

DIVE GROUP

WEATHER CONDITIONS

START
bar / psi

END
bar / psi

LOCATION

TIME IN

TIME OUT

: :

DIVE TIME

:

AVERAGE DEPTH

MAX DEPTH

ADDITIONAL NOTES

WEATHER CONDITIONS

LOCATION

LOCATION NAME

COUNTRY

EQUIPMENT

DIVE CENTER / RESORT STAMP

INSTRUCTOR   AI / DM   BUDDY

DIVE NO

DATE

DIVE GROUP

WEATHER CONDITIONS

WEATHER CONDITIONS

START
bar / psi

END
bar / psi

LOCATION

TIME IN

TIME OUT

:

:

DIVE TIME

:

AVERAGE DEPTH

MAX DEPTH

LOCATION

LOCATION NAME

COUNTRY

EQUIPMENT

ADDITIONAL NOTES

DIVE CENTER / RESORT STAMP

INSTRUCTOR

AI / DM

BUDDY

DIVE NO

DATE

DIVE GROUP

WEATHER CONDITIONS

	START bar / psi		END bar / psi
	_____		_____

LOCATION

TIME IN

:

TIME OUT

:

DIVE TIME

:

AVERAGE DEPTH

MAX DEPTH

ADDITIONAL NOTES

WEATHER CONDITIONS

☀ ⛅ 🌧 ⛈ ❄

☐ ☐ ☐ ☐ ☐

LOCATION

LOCATION NAME

COUNTRY

EQUIPMENT

DIVE CENTER / RESORT STAMP

INSTRUCTOR	AI / DM	BUDDY
☐	☐	☐

DIVE NO

DATE

DIVE GROUP

WEATHER CONDITIONS

WEATHER CONDITIONS

START
bar / psi

END
bar / psi

LOCATION

TIME IN

TIME OUT

DIVE TIME

AVERAGE DEPTH

MAX DEPTH

LOCATION

LOCATION NAME

COUNTRY

EQUIPMENT

ADDITIONAL NOTES

DIVE CENTER / RESORT STAMP

INSTRUCTOR

AI / DM

BUDDY

DIVE NO

DATE

DIVE GROUP

WEATHER CONDITIONS

WEATHER CONDITIONS

START
bar / psi

END
bar / psi

LOCATION

TIME IN   TIME OUT
:   :

DIVE TIME
:

AVERAGE DEPTH

MAX DEPTH

LOCATION

LOCATION NAME

COUNTRY

EQUIPMENT

ADDITIONAL NOTES

DIVE CENTER / RESORT STAMP

INSTRUCTOR   AI / DM   BUDDY

	DIVE NO
	DATE
	DIVE GROUP

WEATHER CONDITIONS

Temperature ___ ☀ ⛅ 🌧 ⛈ ❄
Wind ___ ☐ ☐ ☐ ☐ ☐

WEATHER CONDITIONS

START bar / psi ___	END bar / psi ___

LOCATION

TIME IN   TIME OUT
:   :

DIVE TIME
:

	AVERAGE DEPTH
	MAX DEPTH

LOCATION

	LOCATION NAME
	COUNTRY

EQUIPMENT

ADDITIONAL NOTES

DIVE CENTER / RESORT STAMP

INSTRUCTOR   AI / DM   BUDDY
☐   ☐   ☐

DIVE NO

DATE

DIVE GROUP

WEATHER CONDITIONS

— ☼ ⛅ 🌧 ⛈ ❄

— ☐ ☐ ☐ ☐ ☐

WEATHER CONDITIONS

START bar / psi		END bar / psi
_____		_____

LOCATION

LOCATION NAME

COUNTRY

LOCATION

TIME IN   TIME OUT

:   :

DIVE TIME

:

AVERAGE DEPTH

MAX DEPTH

EQUIPMENT

ADDITIONAL NOTES

DIVE CENTER / RESORT STAMP

INSTRUCTOR   AI / DM   BUDDY

☐   ☐   ☐

DIVE NO

DATE

DIVE GROUP

WEATHER CONDITIONS

WEATHER CONDITIONS

START
bar / psi

END
bar / psi

LOCATION

TIME IN

TIME OUT

:

:

DIVE TIME

:

AVERAGE DEPTH

MAX DEPTH

LOCATION

LOCATION NAME

COUNTRY

EQUIPMENT

ADDITIONAL NOTES

DIVE CENTER / RESORT STAMP

INSTRUCTOR

AI / DM

BUDDY

DIVE NO

DATE

DIVE GROUP

WEATHER CONDITIONS

	—	☼	⛅	🌧	⛈	❄
	—	☐	☐	☐	☐	☐

WEATHER CONDITIONS

START bar / psi	END bar / psi
____	____

LOCATION

TIME IN	TIME OUT
:	:

DIVE TIME

:

AVERAGE DEPTH

MAX DEPTH

LOCATION

LOCATION NAME

COUNTRY

EQUIPMENT

ADDITIONAL NOTES

DIVE CENTER / RESORT STAMP

INSTRUCTOR	AI / DM	BUDDY
☐	☐	☐

🤿 **DIVE NO**	
📅 **DATE**	
👥 **DIVE GROUP**	

WEATHER CONDITIONS

🌡️ _____ ☀️ ⛅ 🌧️ ⛈️ ❄️

🚩 _____ ☐ ☐ ☐ ☐ ☐

WEATHER CONDITIONS

START bar / psi _____

END bar / psi _____

LOCATION

TIME IN _____ : _____ TIME OUT _____ : _____

DIVE TIME _____ : _____

∅ AVERAGE DEPTH

↓ MAX DEPTH

LOCATION

📍 LOCATION NAME

🗺️ COUNTRY

EQUIPMENT

ADDITIONAL NOTES

DIVE CENTER / RESORT STAMP

INSTRUCTOR ☐   AI / DM ☐   BUDDY ☐

DIVE NO

DATE

DIVE GROUP

WEATHER CONDITIONS

	START bar / psi		END bar / psi

LOCATION

TIME IN

TIME OUT

:

:

DIVE TIME

:

AVERAGE DEPTH

MAX DEPTH

ADDITIONAL NOTES

WEATHER CONDITIONS

LOCATION

LOCATION NAME

COUNTRY

EQUIPMENT

DIVE CENTER / RESORT STAMP

INSTRUCTOR   AI / DM   BUDDY

DIVE NO

DATE

DIVE GROUP

WEATHER CONDITIONS

START
bar / psi

END
bar / psi

LOCATION

TIME IN

TIME OUT

:

:

DIVE TIME

:

AVERAGE DEPTH

MAX DEPTH

WEATHER CONDITIONS

LOCATION

LOCATION NAME

COUNTRY

EQUIPMENT

ADDITIONAL NOTES

DIVE CENTER / RESORT STAMP

INSTRUCTOR

AI / DM

BUDDY

DIVE NO

DATE

DIVE GROUP

WEATHER CONDITIONS

START
bar / psi

END
bar / psi

LOCATION

TIME IN

TIME OUT

:

:

DIVE TIME

:

AVERAGE DEPTH

MAX DEPTH

WEATHER CONDITIONS

LOCATION

LOCATION NAME

COUNTRY

EQUIPMENT

ADDITIONAL NOTES

DIVE CENTER / RESORT STAMP

INSTRUCTOR

AI / DM

BUDDY

DIVE NO

DATE

DIVE GROUP

WEATHER CONDITIONS

START
bar / psi
_____

END
bar / psi
_____

LOCATION

TIME IN   TIME OUT
  :   :

DIVE TIME
  :

AVERAGE DEPTH

MAX DEPTH

WEATHER CONDITIONS

_____

_____

LOCATION

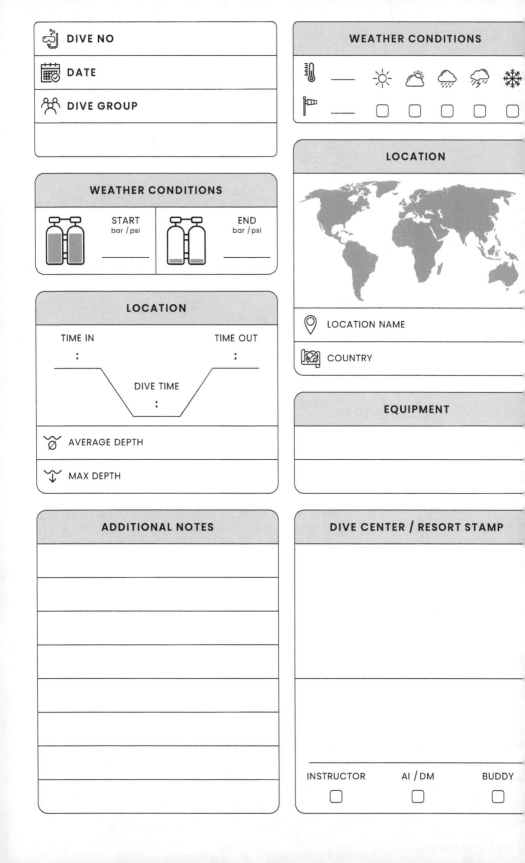

LOCATION NAME

COUNTRY

EQUIPMENT

ADDITIONAL NOTES

DIVE CENTER / RESORT STAMP

INSTRUCTOR   AI / DM   BUDDY

DIVE NO

DATE

DIVE GROUP

WEATHER CONDITIONS

	START bar / psi		END bar / psi

LOCATION

TIME IN

TIME OUT

:   :

DIVE TIME

:

AVERAGE DEPTH

MAX DEPTH

ADDITIONAL NOTES

WEATHER CONDITIONS

LOCATION

LOCATION NAME

COUNTRY

EQUIPMENT

DIVE CENTER / RESORT STAMP

INSTRUCTOR   AI / DM   BUDDY

DIVE NO

DATE

DIVE GROUP

WEATHER CONDITIONS

START bar / psi

END bar / psi

WEATHER CONDITIONS

LOCATION

TIME IN

TIME OUT

DIVE TIME

AVERAGE DEPTH

MAX DEPTH

LOCATION

LOCATION NAME

COUNTRY

EQUIPMENT

ADDITIONAL NOTES

DIVE CENTER / RESORT STAMP

INSTRUCTOR

AI / DM

BUDDY

DIVE NO

DATE

DIVE GROUP

WEATHER CONDITIONS

START
bar / psi

END
bar / psi

LOCATION

TIME IN

TIME OUT

:

:

DIVE TIME

:

AVERAGE DEPTH

MAX DEPTH

ADDITIONAL NOTES

WEATHER CONDITIONS

LOCATION

LOCATION NAME

COUNTRY

EQUIPMENT

DIVE CENTER / RESORT STAMP

INSTRUCTOR   AI / DM   BUDDY

DIVE NO

DATE

DIVE GROUP

WEATHER CONDITIONS

START
bar / psi

____

END
bar / psi

____

LOCATION

TIME IN

:

TIME OUT

:

DIVE TIME

:

AVERAGE DEPTH

MAX DEPTH

WEATHER CONDITIONS

____

____

LOCATION

LOCATION NAME

COUNTRY

EQUIPMENT

ADDITIONAL NOTES

DIVE CENTER / RESORT STAMP

INSTRUCTOR

AI / DM

BUDDY

DIVE NO

DATE

DIVE GROUP

WEATHER CONDITIONS

START
bar / psi
_____

END
bar / psi
_____

LOCATION

TIME IN

TIME OUT

:

:

DIVE TIME

:

AVERAGE DEPTH

MAX DEPTH

ADDITIONAL NOTES

WEATHER CONDITIONS

_____

_____

LOCATION

LOCATION NAME

COUNTRY

EQUIPMENT

DIVE CENTER / RESORT STAMP

INSTRUCTOR   AI / DM   BUDDY

DIVE NO

DATE

DIVE GROUP

WEATHER CONDITIONS

START bar / psi	END bar / psi
_____	_____

LOCATION

TIME IN

:

TIME OUT

:

DIVE TIME

:

AVERAGE DEPTH

MAX DEPTH

ADDITIONAL NOTES

WEATHER CONDITIONS

🌡 ——

🚩 ——

☐ ☐ ☐ ☐ ☐

LOCATION

LOCATION NAME

COUNTRY

EQUIPMENT

DIVE CENTER / RESORT STAMP

INSTRUCTOR	AI / DM	BUDDY
☐	☐	☐

DIVE NO

DATE

DIVE GROUP

WEATHER CONDITIONS

START
bar / psi

END
bar / psi

LOCATION

TIME IN

TIME OUT

:

:

DIVE TIME

:

AVERAGE DEPTH

MAX DEPTH

ADDITIONAL NOTES

WEATHER CONDITIONS

—

—

LOCATION

LOCATION NAME

COUNTRY

EQUIPMENT

DIVE CENTER / RESORT STAMP

INSTRUCTOR   AI / DM   BUDDY

DIVE NO

DATE

DIVE GROUP

WEATHER CONDITIONS

WEATHER CONDITIONS

START
bar / psi

END
bar / psi

LOCATION

LOCATION NAME

COUNTRY

LOCATION

TIME IN

TIME OUT

:

:

DIVE TIME

:

AVERAGE DEPTH

MAX DEPTH

EQUIPMENT

ADDITIONAL NOTES

DIVE CENTER / RESORT STAMP

INSTRUCTOR

AI / DM

BUDDY

DIVE NO

DATE

DIVE GROUP

WEATHER CONDITIONS

——

——

WEATHER CONDITIONS

START bar / psi	END bar / psi

LOCATION

LOCATION NAME

COUNTRY

LOCATION

TIME IN

TIME OUT

DIVE TIME

AVERAGE DEPTH

MAX DEPTH

EQUIPMENT

ADDITIONAL NOTES

DIVE CENTER / RESORT STAMP

INSTRUCTOR   AI / DM   BUDDY

DIVE NO

DATE

DIVE GROUP

WEATHER CONDITIONS

WEATHER CONDITIONS

START
bar / psi

END
bar / psi

LOCATION

LOCATION NAME

COUNTRY

LOCATION

TIME IN

TIME OUT

:

:

DIVE TIME

:

AVERAGE DEPTH

MAX DEPTH

EQUIPMENT

ADDITIONAL NOTES

DIVE CENTER / RESORT STAMP

INSTRUCTOR

AI / DM

BUDDY

DIVE NO

DATE

DIVE GROUP

WEATHER CONDITIONS

WEATHER CONDITIONS

START bar / psi	END bar / psi
_____	_____

LOCATION

TIME IN

:

TIME OUT

:

DIVE TIME

:

AVERAGE DEPTH

MAX DEPTH

LOCATION

LOCATION NAME

COUNTRY

EQUIPMENT

ADDITIONAL NOTES

DIVE CENTER / RESORT STAMP

INSTRUCTOR	AI / DM	BUDDY
☐	☐	☐

DIVE NO

DATE

DIVE GROUP

WEATHER CONDITIONS

START
bar / psi
_____

END
bar / psi
_____

LOCATION

TIME IN   TIME OUT
:   :

DIVE TIME
:

AVERAGE DEPTH

MAX DEPTH

WEATHER CONDITIONS

☐ ☐ ☐ ☐ ☐

LOCATION

LOCATION NAME

COUNTRY

EQUIPMENT

ADDITIONAL NOTES

DIVE CENTER / RESORT STAMP

INSTRUCTOR   AI / DM   BUDDY
☐   ☐   ☐

DIVE NO

DATE

DIVE GROUP

WEATHER CONDITIONS

	START bar / psi		END bar / psi
	_____		_____

LOCATION

TIME IN

:

TIME OUT

:

DIVE TIME

:

AVERAGE DEPTH

MAX DEPTH

ADDITIONAL NOTES

WEATHER CONDITIONS

_____

_____

☐ ☐ ☐ ☐ ☐

LOCATION

📍 LOCATION NAME

🗺 COUNTRY

EQUIPMENT

DIVE CENTER / RESORT STAMP

_____

INSTRUCTOR   AI / DM   BUDDY

☐   ☐   ☐

DIVE NO

DATE

DIVE GROUP

WEATHER CONDITIONS

bar / psi   START

bar / psi   END

WEATHER CONDITIONS

START
bar / psi

_____

END
bar / psi

_____

LOCATION

TIME IN

:

TIME OUT

:

DIVE TIME

:

AVERAGE DEPTH

MAX DEPTH

LOCATION

LOCATION NAME

COUNTRY

EQUIPMENT

ADDITIONAL NOTES

DIVE CENTER / RESORT STAMP

INSTRUCTOR

AI / DM

BUDDY

DIVE NO

DATE

DIVE GROUP

WEATHER CONDITIONS

START
bar / psi

END
bar / psi

LOCATION

TIME IN

TIME OUT

:

:

DIVE TIME

:

AVERAGE DEPTH

MAX DEPTH

ADDITIONAL NOTES

WEATHER CONDITIONS

LOCATION

LOCATION NAME

COUNTRY

EQUIPMENT

DIVE CENTER / RESORT STAMP

INSTRUCTOR

AI / DM

BUDDY

DIVE NO

DATE

DIVE GROUP

WEATHER CONDITIONS

WEATHER CONDITIONS

START
bar / psi

END
bar / psi

LOCATION

LOCATION NAME

COUNTRY

LOCATION

TIME IN

TIME OUT

:

:

DIVE TIME

:

AVERAGE DEPTH

MAX DEPTH

EQUIPMENT

ADDITIONAL NOTES

DIVE CENTER / RESORT STAMP

INSTRUCTOR

AI / DM

BUDDY

DIVE NO

DATE

DIVE GROUP

WEATHER CONDITIONS

WEATHER CONDITIONS

START
bar / psi

END
bar / psi

LOCATION

TIME IN

TIME OUT

:

:

DIVE TIME

:

AVERAGE DEPTH

MAX DEPTH

LOCATION

LOCATION NAME

COUNTRY

EQUIPMENT

ADDITIONAL NOTES

DIVE CENTER / RESORT STAMP

INSTRUCTOR   AI / DM   BUDDY

DIVE NO

DATE

DIVE GROUP

WEATHER CONDITIONS

START
bar / psi
____

END
bar / psi
____

LOCATION

TIME IN   TIME OUT
:   :

DIVE TIME
:

AVERAGE DEPTH

MAX DEPTH

WEATHER CONDITIONS

LOCATION

LOCATION NAME

COUNTRY

EQUIPMENT

ADDITIONAL NOTES

DIVE CENTER / RESORT STAMP

INSTRUCTOR   AI / DM   BUDDY

DIVE NO

DATE

DIVE GROUP

WEATHER CONDITIONS

WEATHER CONDITIONS

	START bar / psi		END bar / psi
	_____		_____

LOCATION

TIME IN   TIME OUT
:   :

DIVE TIME
:

AVERAGE DEPTH

MAX DEPTH

LOCATION

LOCATION NAME

COUNTRY

EQUIPMENT

ADDITIONAL NOTES

DIVE CENTER / RESORT STAMP

_____

INSTRUCTOR   AI / DM   BUDDY

DIVE NO

DATE

DIVE GROUP

WEATHER CONDITIONS

WEATHER CONDITIONS

START
bar / psi

END
bar / psi

LOCATION

TIME IN

TIME OUT

:

:

DIVE TIME

:

AVERAGE DEPTH

MAX DEPTH

LOCATION

LOCATION NAME

COUNTRY

EQUIPMENT

ADDITIONAL NOTES

DIVE CENTER / RESORT STAMP

INSTRUCTOR

AI / DM

BUDDY

DIVE NO

DATE

DIVE GROUP

WEATHER CONDITIONS

WEATHER CONDITIONS

START
bar / psi

END
bar / psi

LOCATION

TIME IN

TIME OUT

:

:

DIVE TIME

:

AVERAGE DEPTH

MAX DEPTH

LOCATION

LOCATION NAME

COUNTRY

EQUIPMENT

ADDITIONAL NOTES

DIVE CENTER / RESORT STAMP

INSTRUCTOR

AI / DM

BUDDY

DIVE NO

DATE

DIVE GROUP

WEATHER CONDITIONS

WEATHER CONDITIONS

START
bar / psi

END
bar / psi

LOCATION

TIME IN

TIME OUT

:

:

DIVE TIME

:

AVERAGE DEPTH

MAX DEPTH

LOCATION

LOCATION NAME

COUNTRY

EQUIPMENT

ADDITIONAL NOTES

DIVE CENTER / RESORT STAMP

INSTRUCTOR

AI / DM

BUDDY

DIVE NO

DATE

DIVE GROUP

WEATHER CONDITIONS

WEATHER CONDITIONS

START
bar / psi

END
bar / psi

____

____

LOCATION

TIME IN

TIME OUT

:

:

DIVE TIME

:

AVERAGE DEPTH

MAX DEPTH

LOCATION

LOCATION NAME

COUNTRY

EQUIPMENT

ADDITIONAL NOTES

DIVE CENTER / RESORT STAMP

INSTRUCTOR

AI / DM

BUDDY

DIVE NO

DATE

DIVE GROUP

WEATHER CONDITIONS

START
bar / psi
_____

END
bar / psi
_____

WEATHER CONDITIONS

_____

_____

LOCATION

TIME IN

TIME OUT

:

:

DIVE TIME

:

AVERAGE DEPTH

MAX DEPTH

LOCATION

LOCATION NAME

COUNTRY

EQUIPMENT

ADDITIONAL NOTES

DIVE CENTER / RESORT STAMP

INSTRUCTOR

AI / DM

BUDDY

DIVE NO

DATE

DIVE GROUP

WEATHER CONDITIONS

START
bar / psi

END
bar / psi

WEATHER CONDITIONS

LOCATION

TIME IN

TIME OUT

:

:

DIVE TIME

:

AVERAGE DEPTH

MAX DEPTH

LOCATION NAME

COUNTRY

EQUIPMENT

ADDITIONAL NOTES

DIVE CENTER / RESORT STAMP

INSTRUCTOR

AI / DM

BUDDY

DIVE NO

DATE

DIVE GROUP

WEATHER CONDITIONS

WEATHER CONDITIONS

START
bar / psi

END
bar / psi

LOCATION

LOCATION NAME

COUNTRY

LOCATION

TIME IN

TIME OUT

:

:

DIVE TIME

:

AVERAGE DEPTH

MAX DEPTH

EQUIPMENT

ADDITIONAL NOTES

DIVE CENTER / RESORT STAMP

INSTRUCTOR

AI / DM

BUDDY

DIVE NO

DATE

DIVE GROUP

WEATHER CONDITIONS

☀ ⛅ 🌧 ⛈ ❄

WEATHER CONDITIONS

START
bar / psi

END
bar / psi

LOCATION

LOCATION NAME

COUNTRY

LOCATION

TIME IN

TIME OUT

:

:

DIVE TIME

:

AVERAGE DEPTH

MAX DEPTH

EQUIPMENT

ADDITIONAL NOTES

DIVE CENTER / RESORT STAMP

INSTRUCTOR   AI / DM   BUDDY

DIVE NO

DATE

DIVE GROUP

WEATHER CONDITIONS

START
bar / psi

END
bar / psi

LOCATION

TIME IN

:

TIME OUT

:

DIVE TIME

:

AVERAGE DEPTH

MAX DEPTH

WEATHER CONDITIONS

LOCATION

LOCATION NAME

COUNTRY

EQUIPMENT

ADDITIONAL NOTES

DIVE CENTER / RESORT STAMP

INSTRUCTOR

AI / DM

BUDDY

DIVE NO

DATE

DIVE GROUP

WEATHER CONDITIONS

START
bar / psi

END
bar / psi

WEATHER CONDITIONS

LOCATION

TIME IN

TIME OUT

:

:

DIVE TIME

:

AVERAGE DEPTH

MAX DEPTH

LOCATION

LOCATION NAME

COUNTRY

EQUIPMENT

ADDITIONAL NOTES

DIVE CENTER / RESORT STAMP

INSTRUCTOR   AI / DM   BUDDY

DIVE NO

DATE

DIVE GROUP

WEATHER CONDITIONS

START
bar / psi

_____

END
bar / psi

_____

LOCATION

TIME IN

:

TIME OUT

:

DIVE TIME

:

AVERAGE DEPTH

MAX DEPTH

WEATHER CONDITIONS

—

—

LOCATION

LOCATION NAME

COUNTRY

EQUIPMENT

ADDITIONAL NOTES

DIVE CENTER / RESORT STAMP

INSTRUCTOR

AI / DM

BUDDY

DIVE NO

DATE

DIVE GROUP

WEATHER CONDITIONS

	START bar / psi		END bar / psi
	_____		_____

LOCATION

TIME IN

:

TIME OUT

:

DIVE TIME

:

AVERAGE DEPTH

MAX DEPTH

ADDITIONAL NOTES

WEATHER CONDITIONS

🌡 ____   ☀ ⛅ 🌧 ⛈ ❄

🚩 ____   ☐ ☐ ☐ ☐ ☐

LOCATION

LOCATION NAME

COUNTRY

EQUIPMENT

DIVE CENTER / RESORT STAMP

INSTRUCTOR   AI / DM   BUDDY

☐   ☐   ☐

DIVE NO

DATE

DIVE GROUP

WEATHER CONDITIONS

WEATHER CONDITIONS

START
bar / psi

END
bar / psi

LOCATION

TIME IN

TIME OUT

:

:

DIVE TIME

:

AVERAGE DEPTH

MAX DEPTH

LOCATION

LOCATION NAME

COUNTRY

EQUIPMENT

ADDITIONAL NOTES

DIVE CENTER / RESORT STAMP

INSTRUCTOR

AI / DM

BUDDY

DIVE NO

DATE

DIVE GROUP

WEATHER CONDITIONS

🌡	——
🚩	——

☀ 🌤 🌧 ⛈ ❄

☐ ☐ ☐ ☐ ☐

LOCATION

📍 LOCATION NAME

🗺 COUNTRY

WEATHER CONDITIONS

START
bar / psi

_____

END
bar / psi

_____

LOCATION

TIME IN

:

TIME OUT

:

DIVE TIME

:

AVERAGE DEPTH

MAX DEPTH

EQUIPMENT

ADDITIONAL NOTES

DIVE CENTER / RESORT STAMP

_____

INSTRUCTOR   AI / DM   BUDDY

☐   ☐   ☐

DIVE NO

DATE

DIVE GROUP

WEATHER CONDITIONS

🌡 ____	☀ ⛅ 🌧 ⛈ ❄	
🏳 ____	☐ ☐ ☐ ☐ ☐	

WEATHER CONDITIONS

START bar / psi	END bar / psi
____	____

LOCATION

TIME IN   TIME OUT
:   :

DIVE TIME
:

📍 AVERAGE DEPTH

📍 MAX DEPTH

LOCATION

📍 LOCATION NAME

🗺 COUNTRY

EQUIPMENT

ADDITIONAL NOTES

DIVE CENTER / RESORT STAMP

INSTRUCTOR   AI / DM   BUDDY
☐   ☐   ☐

DIVE NO

DATE

DIVE GROUP

WEATHER CONDITIONS

START
bar / psi

END
bar / psi

LOCATION

TIME IN

TIME OUT

:

:

DIVE TIME

:

AVERAGE DEPTH

MAX DEPTH

ADDITIONAL NOTES

WEATHER CONDITIONS

LOCATION

LOCATION NAME

COUNTRY

EQUIPMENT

DIVE CENTER / RESORT STAMP

INSTRUCTOR

AI / DM

BUDDY

DIVE NO

DATE

DIVE GROUP

WEATHER CONDITIONS

WEATHER CONDITIONS

START bar / psi	END bar / psi

LOCATION

TIME IN

TIME OUT

:

:

DIVE TIME

:

AVERAGE DEPTH

MAX DEPTH

LOCATION

LOCATION NAME

COUNTRY

EQUIPMENT

ADDITIONAL NOTES

DIVE CENTER / RESORT STAMP

INSTRUCTOR

AI / DM

BUDDY

DIVE NO

DATE

DIVE GROUP

WEATHER CONDITIONS

🌡 ___   ☀ ⛅ 🌧 ⛈ ❄
🚩 ___   ☐ ☐ ☐ ☐ ☐

WEATHER CONDITIONS

START bar / psi	END bar / psi
___	___

LOCATION

TIME IN	TIME OUT
:	:

DIVE TIME

:

AVERAGE DEPTH

MAX DEPTH

LOCATION

LOCATION NAME

COUNTRY

EQUIPMENT

ADDITIONAL NOTES

DIVE CENTER / RESORT STAMP

_____

INSTRUCTOR   AI / DM   BUDDY

☐   ☐   ☐

DIVE NO

DATE

DIVE GROUP

WEATHER CONDITIONS

START
bar / psi

END
bar / psi

____

____

LOCATION

TIME IN

:

TIME OUT

:

DIVE TIME

:

AVERAGE DEPTH

MAX DEPTH

WEATHER CONDITIONS

____

____

LOCATION

LOCATION NAME

COUNTRY

EQUIPMENT

ADDITIONAL NOTES

DIVE CENTER / RESORT STAMP

INSTRUCTOR

AI / DM

BUDDY

DIVE NO

DATE

DIVE GROUP

WEATHER CONDITIONS

	START bar / psi		END bar / psi
	_____		_____

LOCATION

TIME IN	TIME OUT
:	:

DIVE TIME
:

AVERAGE DEPTH

MAX DEPTH

ADDITIONAL NOTES

WEATHER CONDITIONS

🌡 ___	☀	⛅	🌦	⛈	❄
🚩 ___	☐	☐	☐	☐	☐

LOCATION

LOCATION NAME

COUNTRY

EQUIPMENT

DIVE CENTER / RESORT STAMP

INSTRUCTOR	AI / DM	BUDDY
☐	☐	☐

DIVE NO

DATE

DIVE GROUP

WEATHER CONDITIONS

— ☀ ⛅ 🌧 ⛈ ❄

☐ ☐ ☐ ☐ ☐

WEATHER CONDITIONS

START
bar / psi

END
bar / psi

___

___

LOCATION

LOCATION NAME

COUNTRY

LOCATION

TIME IN   TIME OUT

:   :

DIVE TIME

:

AVERAGE DEPTH

MAX DEPTH

EQUIPMENT

ADDITIONAL NOTES

DIVE CENTER / RESORT STAMP

___

INSTRUCTOR   AI / DM   BUDDY

☐   ☐   ☐

DIVE NO

DATE

DIVE GROUP

WEATHER CONDITIONS

START
bar / psi

END
bar / psi

LOCATION

TIME IN

TIME OUT

:

:

DIVE TIME

:

AVERAGE DEPTH

MAX DEPTH

ADDITIONAL NOTES

WEATHER CONDITIONS

LOCATION

LOCATION NAME

COUNTRY

EQUIPMENT

DIVE CENTER / RESORT STAMP

INSTRUCTOR   AI / DM   BUDDY

DIVE NO

DATE

DIVE GROUP

WEATHER CONDITIONS

WEATHER CONDITIONS

START
bar / psi

_____

END
bar / psi

_____

LOCATION

TIME IN

:

TIME OUT

:

DIVE TIME

:

AVERAGE DEPTH

MAX DEPTH

LOCATION

LOCATION NAME

COUNTRY

EQUIPMENT

ADDITIONAL NOTES

DIVE CENTER / RESORT STAMP

INSTRUCTOR

AI / DM

BUDDY

DIVE NO

DATE

DIVE GROUP

WEATHER CONDITIONS

🌡 —

💨 —

☀️ ⛅ 🌧 ⛈ ❄️

☐ ☐ ☐ ☐ ☐

LOCATION

📍 LOCATION NAME

🗺 COUNTRY

WEATHER CONDITIONS

	START bar / psi		END bar / psi
	___		___

LOCATION

TIME IN

:

TIME OUT

:

DIVE TIME

:

AVERAGE DEPTH

MAX DEPTH

EQUIPMENT

ADDITIONAL NOTES

DIVE CENTER / RESORT STAMP

INSTRUCTOR   AI / DM   BUDDY

☐   ☐   ☐

DIVE NO

DATE

DIVE GROUP

WEATHER CONDITIONS

WEATHER CONDITIONS

START
bar / psi

END
bar / psi

LOCATION

TIME IN

TIME OUT

:

:

DIVE TIME

:

AVERAGE DEPTH

MAX DEPTH

LOCATION

LOCATION NAME

COUNTRY

EQUIPMENT

ADDITIONAL NOTES

DIVE CENTER / RESORT STAMP

INSTRUCTOR

AI / DM

BUDDY

DIVE NO

DATE

DIVE GROUP

WEATHER CONDITIONS

START bar / psi	END bar / psi
_____	_____

LOCATION

TIME IN

:

TIME OUT

:

DIVE TIME

:

AVERAGE DEPTH

MAX DEPTH

ADDITIONAL NOTES

WEATHER CONDITIONS

☀ ⛅ 🌧 ⛈ ❄
☐ ☐ ☐ ☐ ☐

LOCATION

LOCATION NAME

COUNTRY

EQUIPMENT

DIVE CENTER / RESORT STAMP

INSTRUCTOR   AI / DM   BUDDY
☐   ☐   ☐

DIVE NO

DATE

DIVE GROUP

WEATHER CONDITIONS

START
bar / psi

END
bar / psi

LOCATION

TIME IN

TIME OUT

:

:

DIVE TIME

:

AVERAGE DEPTH

MAX DEPTH

WEATHER CONDITIONS

LOCATION

LOCATION NAME

COUNTRY

EQUIPMENT

ADDITIONAL NOTES

DIVE CENTER / RESORT STAMP

INSTRUCTOR

AI / DM

BUDDY

DIVE NO

DATE

DIVE GROUP

WEATHER CONDITIONS

START
bar / psi

END
bar / psi

LOCATION

TIME IN

TIME OUT

:

:

DIVE TIME

:

AVERAGE DEPTH

MAX DEPTH

ADDITIONAL NOTES

WEATHER CONDITIONS

LOCATION

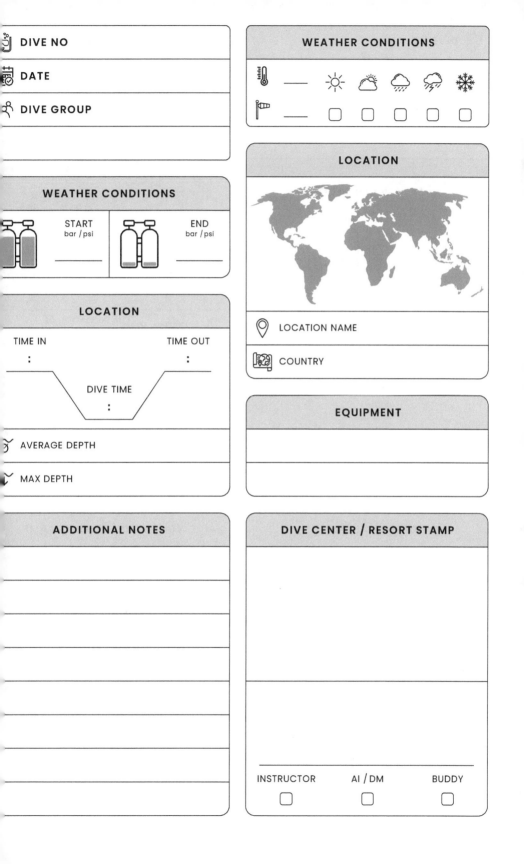

LOCATION NAME

COUNTRY

EQUIPMENT

DIVE CENTER / RESORT STAMP

INSTRUCTOR

AI / DM

BUDDY

DIVE NO

DATE

DIVE GROUP

WEATHER CONDITIONS

START
bar / psi

END
bar / psi

_____

_____

LOCATION

TIME IN

TIME OUT

:

:

DIVE TIME

:

AVERAGE DEPTH

MAX DEPTH

WEATHER CONDITIONS

____

____

LOCATION

LOCATION NAME

COUNTRY

EQUIPMENT

ADDITIONAL NOTES

DIVE CENTER / RESORT STAMP

INSTRUCTOR

AI / DM

BUDDY

DIVE NO

DATE

DIVE GROUP

WEATHER CONDITIONS

START
bar / psi

END
bar / psi

LOCATION

TIME IN

TIME OUT

:

:

DIVE TIME

:

AVERAGE DEPTH

MAX DEPTH

ADDITIONAL NOTES

WEATHER CONDITIONS

—

—

LOCATION

LOCATION NAME

COUNTRY

EQUIPMENT

DIVE CENTER / RESORT STAMP

INSTRUCTOR   AI / DM   BUDDY

DIVE NO

DATE

DIVE GROUP

WEATHER CONDITIONS

START
bar / psi

END
bar / psi

LOCATION

TIME IN

TIME OUT

:

:

DIVE TIME

:

AVERAGE DEPTH

MAX DEPTH

WEATHER CONDITIONS

LOCATION

LOCATION NAME

COUNTRY

EQUIPMENT

ADDITIONAL NOTES

DIVE CENTER / RESORT STAMP

INSTRUCTOR

AI / DM

BUDDY

DIVE NO

DATE

DIVE GROUP

WEATHER CONDITIONS

START bar / psi _____

END bar / psi _____

LOCATION

TIME IN

TIME OUT

:   :

DIVE TIME

:

AVERAGE DEPTH

MAX DEPTH

ADDITIONAL NOTES

WEATHER CONDITIONS

LOCATION

LOCATION NAME

COUNTRY

EQUIPMENT

DIVE CENTER / RESORT STAMP

INSTRUCTOR   AI / DM   BUDDY

DIVE NO

DATE

DIVE GROUP

WEATHER CONDITIONS

START bar / psi

END bar / psi

LOCATION

TIME IN

TIME OUT

:

:

DIVE TIME

:

AVERAGE DEPTH

MAX DEPTH

WEATHER CONDITIONS

LOCATION

LOCATION NAME

COUNTRY

EQUIPMENT

ADDITIONAL NOTES

DIVE CENTER / RESORT STAMP

INSTRUCTOR

AI / DM

BUDDY

DIVE NO

DATE

DIVE GROUP

WEATHER CONDITIONS

	START bar / psi		END bar / psi

LOCATION

TIME IN

TIME OUT

:

:

DIVE TIME

:

AVERAGE DEPTH

MAX DEPTH

ADDITIONAL NOTES

WEATHER CONDITIONS

☐ ☐ ☐ ☐ ☐

LOCATION

📍 LOCATION NAME

🗺️ COUNTRY

EQUIPMENT

DIVE CENTER / RESORT STAMP

INSTRUCTOR	AI / DM	BUDDY
☐	☐	☐

DIVE NO

DATE

DIVE GROUP

WEATHER CONDITIONS

START
bar / psi

END
bar / psi

LOCATION

TIME IN

TIME OUT

:

:

DIVE TIME

:

AVERAGE DEPTH

MAX DEPTH

WEATHER CONDITIONS

LOCATION

LOCATION NAME

COUNTRY

EQUIPMENT

ADDITIONAL NOTES

DIVE CENTER / RESORT STAMP

INSTRUCTOR

AI / DM

BUDDY

DIVE NO

DATE

DIVE GROUP

WEATHER CONDITIONS

WEATHER CONDITIONS

START
bar / psi

END
bar / psi

LOCATION

TIME IN

TIME OUT

:

:

DIVE TIME

:

AVERAGE DEPTH

MAX DEPTH

LOCATION

LOCATION NAME

COUNTRY

EQUIPMENT

ADDITIONAL NOTES

DIVE CENTER / RESORT STAMP

INSTRUCTOR   AI / DM   BUDDY

DIVE NO

DATE

DIVE GROUP

WEATHER CONDITIONS

START
bar / psi
___

END
bar / psi
___

LOCATION

TIME IN   TIME OUT
:   :

DIVE TIME
:

AVERAGE DEPTH

MAX DEPTH

WEATHER CONDITIONS

___

___

LOCATION

LOCATION NAME

COUNTRY

EQUIPMENT

ADDITIONAL NOTES

DIVE CENTER / RESORT STAMP

INSTRUCTOR   AI / DM   BUDDY

DIVE NO

DATE

DIVE GROUP

WEATHER CONDITIONS

☀ ⛅ 🌧 ⛈ ❄

WEATHER CONDITIONS

START bar / psi	END bar / psi

LOCATION

LOCATION NAME

COUNTRY

LOCATION

TIME IN   TIME OUT
:   :

DIVE TIME
:

AVERAGE DEPTH

MAX DEPTH

EQUIPMENT

ADDITIONAL NOTES

DIVE CENTER / RESORT STAMP

INSTRUCTOR   AI / DM   BUDDY

DIVE NO

DATE

DIVE GROUP

WEATHER CONDITIONS

START
bar / psi

_____

END
bar / psi

_____

LOCATION

TIME IN

:

TIME OUT

:

DIVE TIME

:

AVERAGE DEPTH

MAX DEPTH

WEATHER CONDITIONS

_____

_____

☐ ☐ ☐ ☐ ☐

LOCATION

LOCATION NAME

COUNTRY

EQUIPMENT

ADDITIONAL NOTES

DIVE CENTER / RESORT STAMP

INSTRUCTOR   AI / DM   BUDDY

☐   ☐   ☐

DIVE NO

DATE

DIVE GROUP

WEATHER CONDITIONS

START bar / psi	END bar / psi
_____	_____

LOCATION

TIME IN

:

TIME OUT

:

DIVE TIME

:

AVERAGE DEPTH

MAX DEPTH

ADDITIONAL NOTES

WEATHER CONDITIONS

—

—

☐ ☐ ☐ ☐ ☐

LOCATION

LOCATION NAME

COUNTRY

EQUIPMENT

DIVE CENTER / RESORT STAMP

INSTRUCTOR ☐   AI / DM ☐   BUDDY ☐

DIVE NO

DATE

DIVE GROUP

WEATHER CONDITIONS

START
bar / psi

_____

END
bar / psi

_____

WEATHER CONDITIONS

_____

_____

LOCATION

TIME IN   TIME OUT
:   :

DIVE TIME
:

AVERAGE DEPTH

MAX DEPTH

LOCATION

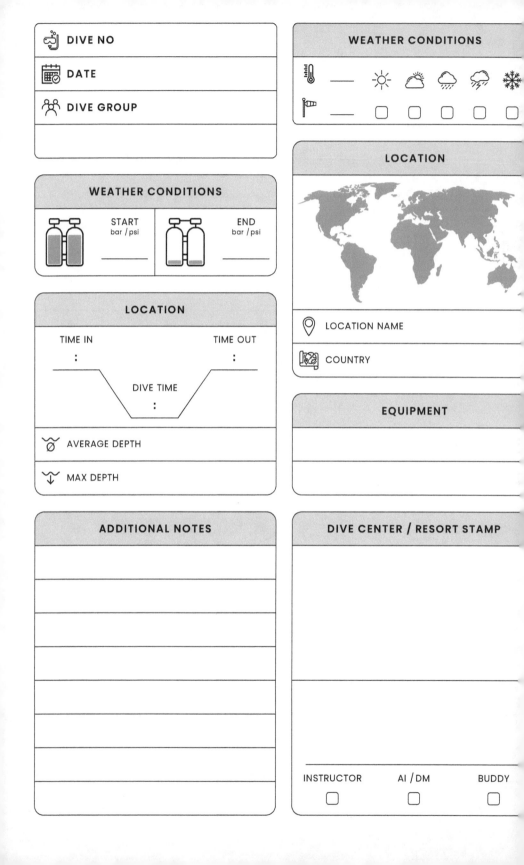

LOCATION NAME

COUNTRY

EQUIPMENT

ADDITIONAL NOTES

DIVE CENTER / RESORT STAMP

INSTRUCTOR   AI / DM   BUDDY

DIVE NO

DATE

DIVE GROUP

WEATHER CONDITIONS

☐ ☐ ☐ ☐ ☐

WEATHER CONDITIONS

START bar / psi	END bar / psi
_____	_____

LOCATION

📍 LOCATION NAME

🗺 COUNTRY

LOCATION

TIME IN   TIME OUT
:   :

DIVE TIME
:

AVERAGE DEPTH

MAX DEPTH

EQUIPMENT

ADDITIONAL NOTES

DIVE CENTER / RESORT STAMP

INSTRUCTOR   AI / DM   BUDDY
☐   ☐   ☐

DIVE NO

DATE

DIVE GROUP

WEATHER CONDITIONS

	START bar / psi		END bar / psi
	_____		_____

LOCATION

TIME IN

:

TIME OUT

:

DIVE TIME

:

AVERAGE DEPTH

MAX DEPTH

ADDITIONAL NOTES

WEATHER CONDITIONS

LOCATION

LOCATION NAME

COUNTRY

EQUIPMENT

DIVE CENTER / RESORT STAMP

INSTRUCTOR   AI / DM   BUDDY

DIVE NO

DATE

DIVE GROUP

WEATHER CONDITIONS

🌡 ——	☀	⛅	🌧	⛈	❄
🚩 ——	☐	☐	☐	☐	☐

WEATHER CONDITIONS

START
bar / psi

_____

END
bar / psi

_____

LOCATION

📍 LOCATION NAME

🗺 COUNTRY

LOCATION

TIME IN

:

TIME OUT

:

DIVE TIME

:

AVERAGE DEPTH

MAX DEPTH

EQUIPMENT

ADDITIONAL NOTES

DIVE CENTER / RESORT STAMP

INSTRUCTOR	AI / DM	BUDDY
☐	☐	☐

DIVE NO

DATE

DIVE GROUP

WEATHER CONDITIONS

START
bar / psi

END
bar / psi

LOCATION

TIME IN

TIME OUT

:

:

DIVE TIME

:

AVERAGE DEPTH

MAX DEPTH

ADDITIONAL NOTES

WEATHER CONDITIONS

LOCATION

LOCATION NAME

COUNTRY

EQUIPMENT

DIVE CENTER / RESORT STAMP

INSTRUCTOR   AI / DM   BUDDY

DIVE NO

DATE

DIVE GROUP

WEATHER CONDITIONS

START bar / psi	END bar / psi
_____	_____

LOCATION

TIME IN

:

TIME OUT

:

DIVE TIME

:

AVERAGE DEPTH

MAX DEPTH

ADDITIONAL NOTES

WEATHER CONDITIONS

LOCATION

LOCATION NAME

COUNTRY

EQUIPMENT

DIVE CENTER / RESORT STAMP

INSTRUCTOR   AI / DM   BUDDY

DIVE NO

DATE

DIVE GROUP

WEATHER CONDITIONS

WEATHER CONDITIONS

START
bar / psi

_____

END
bar / psi

_____

LOCATION

TIME IN

:

TIME OUT

:

DIVE TIME

:

AVERAGE DEPTH

MAX DEPTH

LOCATION

LOCATION NAME

COUNTRY

EQUIPMENT

ADDITIONAL NOTES

DIVE CENTER / RESORT STAMP

INSTRUCTOR

AI / DM

BUDDY

DIVE NO

DATE

DIVE GROUP

WEATHER CONDITIONS

☀ ⛅ 🌧 ⛈ ❄

WEATHER CONDITIONS

	START bar / psi		END bar / psi

LOCATION

TIME IN :   TIME OUT :

DIVE TIME :

AVERAGE DEPTH

MAX DEPTH

LOCATION

LOCATION NAME

COUNTRY

EQUIPMENT

ADDITIONAL NOTES

DIVE CENTER / RESORT STAMP

INSTRUCTOR   AI / DM   BUDDY

Made in United States
Troutdale, OR
05/03/2024